THE
NEW TESTAMENT
DEACON

STUDY GUIDE

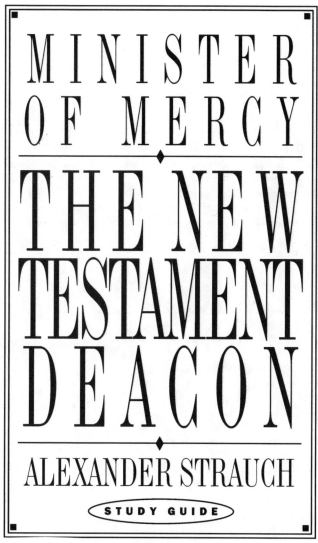

MINISTER OF MERCY

THE NEW TESTAMENT DEACON

ALEXANDER STRAUCH

STUDY GUIDE

SECOND EDITION

LEWIS & ROTH PUBLISHERS
P. O. Box 469, Littleton, CO 80160
www.lewisandroth.com

THE AUTHOR

Alexander Strauch and his wife, Marilyn, reside in Littleton, Colorado, near their four married daughters. Mr. Strauch is a gifted Bible teacher and an elder at a church in Littleton where he has served for over 30 years. Other works by Mr. Strauch include: *Biblical Eldership, The New Testament Deacon, Agape Leadership, Men and Women: Equal Yet Different,* and *Meetings That Work.*

The New Testament Deacon Study Guide
ISBN: 0-93608-310-7
© 1992, 1994 by Alexander Strauch. All rights reserved.

Editors: Stephen and Amanda Sorenson
Cover Design: Stephen T. Eames (www.EamesCreative.com)

All Scripture quotations, except those noted otherwise, are from the NEW AMERICAN STANDARD BIBLE, ©1960, 1963, 1968, 1972, 1973, 1975, 1977, and 1995 by The Lockman Foundation. Used by permission.

Printed in the United States of America
Ninth Printing / 2006

To receive a **free catalog** of books published by Lewis & Roth Publishers, call toll free: **800-477-3239**. If you are calling from outside the United States, please call 719-494-1800.

Lewis & Roth Publishers
P.O. Box 469
Littleton, CO 80160
www.lewisandroth.com

Contents

Special thanks

—— *to* ——

Brad Soukup and John Pitzer

for their help in preparing
this Second Edition.

The Aims of This Guidebook

This guidebook is designed to be used by deacons, wives of deacons, and deacons in training. It can be studied individually or with a group.

There are six lessons. If you are studying with a group, plan to do one lesson a month. I would strongly suggest that you read through the entire book, *The New Testament Deacon*, before starting the guidebook. I say this because the guide does not follow the book chapter by chapter; the guidebook is organized topically. The guide requires you to read only sections of the book.

The first purpose of this guidebook is to help God's people think more biblically about the diaconate as it relates to the life of the church and to needy people.

Only when people are taught by God-breathed Scripture and the illuminating power of the Holy Spirit can they be rightly motivated and educated toward helping people in need. Working with people's problems, needs, and hurts is tough business. It demands strong commitment, deep resources of love, God-given wisdom, extraordinary tact, and supernatural strength.

Many people quickly burn out or become discouraged when they commit themselves to help poor and needy people. So if you expect to persevere and please God in your service, you must be properly motivated and educated.

You must know God's principles and ways. You must know what He requires of those who would serve Him and what He thinks of the needy. You must take on His heart and perspective on people. You must know how to draw upon His strength and comfort. Such knowledge can only be acquired by prayerful study of God's book, the holy Scriptures.

In order to accomplish our first purpose, we will explore many portions of Scripture. To make work easier for you, I have quoted most of the Scripture passages you are required to read. I have used the *New American Standard Bible.*

The second purpose of this guidebook is to give practical ideas for implementing a New Testament diaconate in your local church.

The guide will provide many stimulating questions, practical suggestions, assignments, and warnings. These are meant to help improve your diaconate or to get it started. Some of the assignments and suggestions may not be relevant to your local church situation, so feel free to skip over those that are not applicable.

Please do not rush through the suggestions and assignments, however. As you meet together to discuss these questions, assignments, and suggestions, fresh ideas will emerge for improving your diaconate and ministry to people. Appoint a study leader for each lesson who will limit the discussion time. One controversial question or work assignment, for example, could take hours to discuss, so someone needs to limit the amount of time devoted to each question.

If an assignment or suggestion requires far greater in-depth discussion or planning than time allows, save it until later so that sufficient discussion and thought can take place. *Record these postponed discussions on the pages at the back of the book entitled "Future Discussion Planning Sheet." When you complete the study guide, list the postponed items in priority order and schedule time to work on each one.*

A Word of Encouragement

Some questions will expose gaping inadequacies and needs in your diaconate. At times you may feel overwhelmed by the task ahead of you, but do not let discouragement defeat you. Discouragement is one of the worst enemies of the soul. Ask God to help you be persistent in the face of problems and setbacks. Remember the encouraging words of our Lord that we "ought to pray and not...lose heart" (Luke 18:1).

It takes many years to develop a mature, strong diaconate, and you can only realistically deal with one or two major changes at a time. So be patient, but not passive.

Throughout the guidebook I recommend books to read or to have available for others to read. In recommending these books, however, I am not endorsing everything written in these books. But these books provide excellent ideas and helps for those who would serve through deaconal service. So in the words of Scripture, "examine everything carefully; hold fast to that which is good, abstain from every form of evil" (1 Thessalonians 5:21,22).

"I was sick, and you visited Me"

Matthew 25:36*b*

LESSON 1

FACING THE ISSUES
(Read pages 8-12)

Have you completed reading *The New Testament Deacon* in its entirety? If not, please read the book before doing lesson two.

1. Before reading *The New Testament Deacon*, what was (or is) your idea of a church deacon?

_____

_____

_____

2. According to the preface entitled, "Facing The Issues," what basic, foundational problem exists with the way that many churches think about the deacons' ministry? What much bigger problem is this one merely a symptom of?

_____

_____

_____

_____

_____

3. This problem has given rise to some unbiblical (and unhelpful) models of what the deacon ministry is. What are they and what are some harmful results of them?

_____

_____

_____

_____

WHAT DO DEACONS DO?
(Read pages 25-34; 71-76)

4. To be effective for God, deacons must clearly understand their identity and function in the body. How does the Greek word for deacon, _diakonos_, help you better understand your work and identity? (See Professor Cranfield's two quotations on _diakonos_ on pages 48 and 73. Do you understand what he is saying?)

_____

_____

_____

_____

5. In specific terms, what does the Acts 6:1-6 account teach you about deacons' duties?

_____

_____

_____

_____

6. Since all Christians are called to serve one another and to use their spiritual gifts, why does the local church need the office of deacon? (See pages 42,43.)

_____

_____

_____

_____

_____

_____

7. From the qualifications listed in 1 Timothy 3:8-12, what do we learn about what deacons ought to be and do and what do we learn about what they ought not to be and do? (See also pages 89,90.)

_____

_____

_____

_____

_____

8. What does the Bible mean by the word *mercy?* What do we mean by the term *mercy ministries?* (See pages 154-159.)

_____

_____

_____

_____

_____

9. What specifically does your local church do in the way of mercy ministries?

_____

_____

_____

_____

_____

Warning:

Thomas S. Goslin, II writes, "A recent study of 50 congregations indicates that more church dollars are being spent for utilities and correspondingly fewer for benevolences and pastoral services" (*Church Without Walls,* [Pasadena: Hope Publishing House, 1984], p. 35,36).

If your congregation owns a church building, you must be aware that building maintenance and costs can absorb all your time, thought, and money. In most churches where the deacons are responsible for the church building, building maintenance and supervision inevitably consumes most of their time and money.

Therefore, I recommend that the elders of the church require the deacons to set up a separate building maintenance committee to be responsible for the building. Of course, in a small church some of the deacons or elders may have to serve on that committee. But the sooner the building committee can operate without them the better. Do not allow your diaconate to become simply a building maintenance committee or church finance committee.

10. What do you think about the above counsel? (See page 157.) How might this recommendation be implemented in your church?

_____

_____

_____

_____

_____

Assignments:

1) Establish a widows' list and review it regularly. By either calling or visiting, collect pertinent information regarding the welfare of every widow in your local church. Keep this information on file and confidential.

2) Establish a list of those who are chronically sick or disabled and review it regularly. Care for these people will involve many helpers and require effective follow-up.

3) Establish a list of all who are unable to attend services because of physical or emotional problems. Regular contact with shut-ins needs to be maintained. They should receive tapes of the Sunday morning messages and church bulletins. Through visits, calls, and special services held in their homes, they will know that they are not forgotten.

4) Establish a list of all who suffer from financial difficulties. This list should especially identify single parents and those who are unemployed.

5) Establish a list of all other duties that the shepherds expect you to handle and outline what is involved in fulfilling each of those responsibilities.

Scripture Memory Assignment:

James 1:27

"I was hungry, and you gave Me something to eat"

Matthew 25:35*a*

LESSON 2

Review and discuss the assignments given in lesson one. If any assignment or suggestion demands more discussion or planning time than you have available during your study session, place it on the "Future Discussion Planning Sheet" on page 87.

PLURALITY OF DEACONS

1. Pages 91 and 92 enumerate four reasons for the necessity of a plurality of deacons. In your opinion, which two of the four points are most important for explaining why we need a plurality of deacons?

_____

_____

_____

2. In light of the four reasons for a plurality of deacons, it is obvious that deacons need to meet regularly as a group. If deacons don't meet regularly or organize themselves effectively, they inevitably disintegrate as a group and the people who need their help are neglected. Thus we all need the accountability and encouragement that group meetings provide in order to do our work promptly and responsibly.

Discuss how often you as a body of deacons need to meet together and how much time you need for your meetings in order to do your work effectively?

_____

3. The role of chairman (or moderator) in the deacons' meetings is vitally important. The chairman exercises significant control over the direction and efficiency of the meetings. Since a good deal of attention is focused on him during the meetings, considerable thought should be given as to who the chairman should be and the manner in which he ought to conduct his job.

Which leadership characteristics do you believe the chairman should possess? (Not all deacons or shepherds have the ability to chair a meeting with skill, so those who have this ability should take the lead at directing the deacons' or elders' meetings.)

_____

_____

_____

Assignments:

1) Periodically evaluate the tone, order, emphasis, time, and atmosphere of your deacons' meetings. Since your meetings together are vital to the whole church, how may you improve their efficiency and character? Set a date at which time you will evaluate the effectiveness and organization of your meetings together.

I would recommend reading *Making Committees Work* by Mack Tennyson (Zondervan Publishing House, 1992). This book contains many excellent ideas for improving your deacons' meetings. I am not, however, endorsing the church board structure presented in this book.

2) Make sure the deacons' agenda always includes time for each deacon to report on his assignments or problems. This provides a practical means of accountability, a way to determine whether each deacon has accomplished his responsibilities on time. It is also a time to provide help and encouragement to a struggling deacon.

3) Always keep a written record of your weekly assignments and duties. Also set completion dates for the accomplishment of your duties and goals.

THE NECESSITY FOR GOOD MANAGEMENT SKILLS

4. After reading pages 32 and 33, list three reasons why good management skills and disciplines are essential to the diaconate.

_____
_____
_____
_____

5. What potential damage to the church in Jerusalem could have occurred if the Seven had mismanaged the daily distribution of funds to the poor widows?

_____
_____
_____
_____

6. If a deacon is to properly care for his family, serve the church family, and earn a living, he must be self-disciplined. Read the following verses:

> But the fruit of the Spirit is love, joy...self-control (Galatians 5:22a,23a).

> For the overseer must be above reproach as God's steward...hospitable, loving what is good, sensible, just, devout, self-controlled [disciplined] (Titus 1:8).

> And everyone who competes in the games exercises self-control in all things. They then do it to receive a perishable wreath, but we an imperishable. Therefore I run in such a way, as not without aim; I box in such a way, as not beating the air; but I buffet my body and make it my slave, lest possibly, after I have preached to others, I myself should be disqualified (1 Corinthians 9:25-27).

> Like a city that is broken into and without walls Is a man who has no control over his spirit (Proverbs 25:28).

> He who is slow to anger is better than the mighty, And he who rules his spirit, than he who captures a city (Proverbs 16:32).

What do the above verses teach about the biblical doctrine of self-discipline?

_____
_____
_____
_____
_____
_____
_____

Warning: Follow-up and Follow-through

One problem that often plagues deacons is the failure to follow through with assigned duties and tasks. People are hurt and frustrated and the local church is weakened by deacons and elders who procrastinate or forget to do what they are supposed to do.

Here is where the plurality of deacons can help. As a body of deacons, it is important that you honestly and openly discuss this problem regularly. As a body of coworkers, it is important that you learn how to encourage one another, teach and admonish one another, and rebuke one another when needed. The plurality of deacons will not work if you cannot honestly talk with one another, instruct one another, or call one another to account.

Wise people love to be corrected and instructed because they want to grow and improve their character and labors for the Lord. Invite your colleagues to instruct and correct you when needed. As King Solomon said, "Iron sharpens iron, So one man sharpens another" (Proverbs 27:17).

Listen to what the Book of Proverbs says about the wise:

Reprove a wise man, and he will love you,
Give instruction to a wise man, and he will be still wiser,
Teach a righteous man, and he will increase his learning (Proverbs 9:8b,9).

The way of a fool is right in his own eyes,
But a wise man is he who listens to counsel
(Proverbs 12:15).

Whoever loves discipline loves knowledge,
But he who hates reproof is stupid (Proverbs 12:1).

A wise man will hear and increase in learning, And a
man of understanding will acquire wise counsel (Proverbs 1:5).

Pray about this matter now.

THE SHEPHERDS/OVERSEERS
(Read pages 15-24; 57-66)

7. Why is it essential that deacons understand the shepherds' God-given duties and priorities? List at least three reasons. (See pages 16, 21, 23, 58, 66, 77.)

_____
_____
_____
_____
_____

8. From the main passages that deal with elder responsibilities, please make a list of what the biblical duties of the elders are. (Acts 6:1-6; 20:28-35; 1 Timothy 4:14; 5:17,18; Titus 1:9; James 5:14,15; 1 Peter 5:1-4; Hebrews 13:17)

_____
_____
_____
_____
_____
_____

9. Which two passages of Scripture most succinctly explain the New Testament shepherds' work? Why do you think these are good explanations?

_____

_____

_____

_____

_____

10. Among most churches today, which aspect of the shepherds' work is most neglected? Why?

_____

_____

_____

_____

11. What common misconceptions that deacons have about their relationship with the shepherds (overseers) of the local church can lead to conflict? Read pages 77-79.

_____

_____

_____

_____

_____

Warning: The Power of the Purse

A question that often arises is, should the deacons (or trustees) determine the overall financial direction of the church's funds? I would answer "no," because according to Titus 1:7, the elders (not deacons or trustees) are "God's stewards" (Greek, _oikonomos_, "house-manager") of the local church.

The deacons function under the pastoral oversight of the elders (shepherds). The elders delegate responsibility to the deacons, which may include the responsibility to administer the church's funds or just a portion of funds for mercy ministries. However, the final control and direction of the church's funds should be the elders' responsibility.

12. What do you think about this warning? Do you have any recommendations for your local church situation? If you have some good ideas regarding this issue, pass them on to the shepherds of your church.

_____

_____

_____

_____

_____

Practical Suggestions to Discuss:

I can't overstate the importance of implementing good communication principles between shepherds and deacons (and between shepherds and the congregation). Good communication between deacons and shepherds is essential for effective organization and necessary in avoiding conflict. Here are some communication ideas to consider and discuss. Which ideas would you recommend to the elders of your church?

1) Send minutes from elders' meetings to each deacon. Likewise, send minutes from deacons' meetings to each elder.

2) An elder could be present at all deacons' meetings. Likewise, a deacon could be present at all elders' meetings (except when delicate, pastoral matters demand privacy).

3) Schedule an annual elders' and deacons' retreat.

4) Schedule a monthly breakfast between select elders and deacons to discuss problems and direction.

5) Put all official communication between elders and deacons in writing so that communication can be clear and lasting.

Personal Assignment:

1) As an individual deacon, continually seek to improve your personal discipline and life management skills. Here are some good books to read on personal time management:

Charles E. Hummel, *Tyranny of the Urgent*, (Downers Grove: InterVarsity Press, 1977). This is only a fifteen-page booklet, so every deacon should have one.

Ken Smith, *It's About Time: Finding Freedom from Anxiety,* (Wheaton, IL: Crossway Books, 1992). Every deacon should read this book. After you have completed this study guide, study the key chapters of *It's About Time*. You'll find it to be an invaluable resource for improving your personal, life-management skills.

2) You have heard the old saying, "If you want something done, give it to a busy person to do." Seek counsel and practical ideas from productive, well-disciplined people who are successful at personal time management. Learn from their examples.

3) Learn to use the phone effectively to encourage and check on the welfare of hurting people for whom you are responsible. People appreciate a thoughtful, encouraging phone call. They know you can't visit every day, but you can call. When you have a few spare minutes, call a needy person just to say you are thinking about him or her. Pray with that person over the phone. If you do this consistently, you will be amazed by the number of people you can comfort and encourage in a week.

Personal Assignment:

Self-evaluation: Answer each of the following questions as it generally applies to your actions as one member of a team of deacons. Answer with "Y" for "yes," "N" for "no," or "S" for sometimes. You could also include a "+" or "−" next to the "S" in order to be more precise. Do not rush through the questions; honestly evaluate yourself before God. Although this assignment is to be done privately, it would be helpful if another deacon (or your wife) also answered these questions as they pertain to your behavior so you can compare and discuss your answers. (If you are not a deacon, apply these questions to your life situation in which you work closely with others.)

1) I act impulsively and dislike waiting on others for decisions.____

2) I generally trust the judgment of my fellow deacons.___
3) I feel genuine concern for the interests and plans of my fellow workers.___
4) I often act independently of my fellow deacons.___
5) I make myself accountable to my fellow deacons.___
6) I work hard at cooperating with my brethren.___
7) I share my burdens, fears, and problems with my fellow deacons.___
8) I am inclined to carry a grudge.___
9) I am easily frustrated by disagreement.___
10) I am afraid to honestly speak in the deacons' meetings.___
11) I feel free to correct and direct my fellow colleagues.___
12) I actively contribute to discussions and decisions.___
13) I tend to be bossy.___
14) I am too sensitive.___
15) I tend to dominate discussions.___
16) I have a hard time apologizing or admitting I am wrong.___
17) I love my fellow colleagues.___
18) I consciously try to be humble and serve my fellow brethren. ___
19) I pray for my brothers regularly.___

After answering these questions, ask your Father in heaven to give you a true assessment of yourself. Ask Him for the will and power to change your weaknesses or failures that hinder the unity and love of the diaconate.

Scripture Memory Assignment:

Acts 6:2,4

"I was a stranger, and you invited Me in"

Matthew 25:35*c*

LESSON 3

THE NECESSITY FOR CHARACTER QUALIFICATIONS
(Read pages 83-111)

Review and discuss the assignments given in lesson two. If any assignment or suggestion demands more discussion or planning time than you have available during your study session, place it on the "Future Discussion Planning Sheet" on page 87.

1. Define and/or describe what a biblical elder (shepherd) is. Define and/or describe what a biblical deacon is. What is the relationship that should exist between the elders and deacons?

_____

_____

_____

_____

_____

_____

2. First Timothy 3:15 reveals one of the major reasons why Paul wrote the letter of 1 Timothy. Using your own words and those found in *New Testament Deacon*, explain the statement, "I write so that you may know how one ought to conduct himself in the household of God," and how it relates to deacons. (See pages 85-87.)

_____

_____

_____

_____

_____

_____

3. List four reasons why the Bible emphatically insists that deacons be morally and spiritually qualified before they serve.

_____

_____

_____

_____

4. In a word or two, describe what the overall character trait of a deacon should be?

_____

_____

5. In one or two sentences, explain the meaning of this qualification: "Holding to the mystery of the faith with a clear conscience." This is an important qualification, so you need to be clear about what it means.

_____

_____

_____

_____

_____

6. Please review pages 132-136. Give two or three biblical reasons why it is absolutely essential that deacons be holy in the area of sexual relations.

_____

_____

_____

_____

_____

_____

7. Please review pages 141-143 and 1 Timothy 3:12. What is the connection between managing the household and serving the church?

_____

_____

_____

_____

_____

_____

Assignments:

Nearly every year, I hear that someone from a Bible-believing church is caught embezzling church funds. You can be sure that other embezzlers are never caught and that still others steal such small amounts that it is nearly impossible to detect their actions. So it's important that you as a body of deacons, implement careful financial procedures to protect the church from embezzlement. (Again, read pages 32,33.) Do not be naive or unconcerned about this matter. Money often poses a strong temptation even for the best of people.

1) At this time, pray that God will protect you, who carry out the church's ministries of mercy, from financial scandal.

2) Never allow only one person to handle money. At least two people should always count offerings and distribute funds to the needy. Discuss this matter together. Review your financial policies and procedures at least once a year.

3) Here are some recommended books to purchase:

Mack Tennyson, *Church Finances: A Basic Handbook for Church Treasurers, Trustees, Deacons and Ministry Staff* (Zondervan Publishing House)

Richard J. Vargo, *Effective Church Accounting* (Harper and Row Publishers)

Manfred Holck Jr., *Cash Management: Stewardship of the Church's Cash Resources* (Augsburg Fortress Publishers).

4) Practice full disclosure of all your financial accounting. Those who have contributed have a right to know how every dime of their gifts has been used.

8. Remember, a deacon must be a man of wisdom (Acts 6:3). The Book of Proverbs says that a wise man controls his tongue. Prayerfully read the following Proverbs:

When there are many words,
transgression is unavoidable,
But he who restrains his lips is wise
(Proverbs 10:19).

The words of a whisperer are like dainty morsels,
And they go down into the innermost parts of the body
(Proverbs 26:22).

He who goes about as a talebearer reveals secrets,
But he who is trustworthy conceals a matter
(Proverbs 11:13).

As a deacon, you have access to the private lives of people and know confidential information about them and the church. If you are prone to talk too much or to reveal private information, people will lose confidence in you and will not share their problems with you. Your inability to keep confidences will lead to feelings of distrust and ill feeling in the church. Thus you must develop a reputation for confidentiality. This means you must control your tongue.

List some of the tragic results that can come from talking about people in inappropriate ways behind their backs.

_____

_____

_____

WIVES OF DEACONS
(Read pages 112-131)

1 Timothy 3:11 is a highly debated passage. In order to better understand the detailed arguments involved in deciding the correct interpretation, study this section of *The New Testament Deacon* with someone else or the whole body of deacons. Discuss together all the technical points made in chapter 10, on pages 112-126. Discuss these points in a loving, humble Christian manner. Do not fight or become divided over this issue.

9. What was your interpretation of 1 Timothy 3:11 before you read chapter ten in *The New Testament Deacon?*

_____

_____

10. Explain the problem that the Greek word *gynaikas* in 1 Timothy 3:11 creates for the biblical interpreter.

_____

_____

11. Many commentators explain that 1 Timothy 3:11 refers to women who are deacons. List two reasons why they believe verse 11 refers to women deacons.

_____

_____

_____

12. What do you think is the single strongest argument in favor of the interpretation wives of deacons? Explain why.

_____

_____

_____

13. What do you think is the single weakest argument in favor of the interpretion wives of deacons? Explain why.

_____

_____

_____

14. List three examples of how the wife of a deacon can help her deacon husband in diaconal service, assuming you agree with the conclusion stated in NTD.

Warning: Facing Disagreement

Do not divide your church or yourselves over the interpretation of 1 Timothy 3:11. Deal with your differing interpretations in a Christian manner, that is, with patience, love, and humility toward one another. This is a difficult passage to interpret. This issue is not on the same level as the question of whether women can be elders (pastors). Many sound Bible teachers who believe that the eldership of the church is restricted to men teach that women can be deacons. So keep studying, listening, and praying; above all do not allow tempers and egos to get out of control.

Practical Suggestions to Discuss:

1) Encourage the deacons' wives to do this study guide together.

2) Meet occasionally with the deacons' wives for a time of encouragement, idea sharing, problem solving, admonishing, and prayer.

3) Schedule an overnight retreat for deacons and their wives so that you all may enjoy a time of fellowship, brainstorming, and encouragement.

15. List all the essential elements of the process of selecting and examining a deacon for office. (See pages 104-109 of NTD.) Which elements do churches generally neglect today? Why?

_____

_____

_____

_____

_____

16. Why is an official, public installation of deacons important to the church and its officers? (See pages 109-111 of NTD.) How can you improve the process in your church?

_____

_____

_____

_____

Assignment:

Write a diaconal charge that outlines the heart and calling of a deacon. When a deacon is publicly installed into office, read this charge to him in the presence of the whole congregation.

_____

_____

_____

Personal Assignment 1:

Privately evaluate how you stand in light of each qualification below. If you are really brave, ask your wife or a close friend to also evaluate your standing. Circle the two numbers that best represent your present condition.

1) A person worthy of respect

Good   Needs Improvement
_7__6_____5____4_____3___2____1_
                                        Reproachful

2) Not double-tongued

Good   Needs Improvement
_7__6_____5____4_____3___2____1_
                                        Reproachful

3) Not addicted to much wine

Good   Needs Improvement
_7__6_____5____4_____3___2____1_
                                        Reproachful

4) Not fond of sordid gain

Good   Needs Improvement
_7__6_____5____4_____3___2____1_
                                        Reproachful

5) Holding to the mystery of the faith with a clear conscience

Good   Needs Improvement
_7__6_____5____4_____3___2____1_
                                        Reproachful

Personal Assignment for the wives of deacons:

Privately evaluate how you stand in light of each qualification below. If you are really brave, ask your husband or a close friend to evaluate your standing. Circle the two numbers that best represent your present condition.

1) A person worthy of respect

Good   Needs Improvement
__7__6_____5___4_____3___2____1__
                                       Reproachful

2) Not malicious gossips

Good   Needs Improvement
__7__6_____5___4_____3___2____1__
                                       Reproachful

3) Temperate

Good   Needs Improvement
__7__6_____5___4_____3___2____1__
                                       Reproachful

4) Faithful in all things

Good   Needs Improvement
__7__6_____5___4_____3___2____1__
                                       Reproachful

Personal Assignment 2:

Your children are your most precious possessions (Psalms 127:3). It is easy to neglect them because of excessive involvement in church work, but don't. You will pay a heavy price if you do.

Discipline yourself to take time with your children and talk with them. You can discover good, practical ideas from successful fathers or books about being a good father. When I meet good fathers or happy, well-adjusted teenagers, I ask many questions about their home life so that I can improve my own skills as a father.

The following books are good resources for what it means to be a good father and husband:

Joe Temple, *Know Your Child* (Grand Rapids: Baker Book House, 1974).

Kevin Huggins, *Parenting Adolescents* (Colorado Springs: NavPress, 1989).

Ross Campbell, *How to Really Love Your Child* (Victor Books, 1977).

Ross Campbell, *How to Really Love Your Teenager* (Victor Books, 1981).

Dr. James Dobson. Any of his books are excellent reading.

Ed Wheat, M.D., *Love Life: For Every Married Couple* (Grand Rapids: Zondervan Publishing House, 1980).

Gary Smalley, *Love is a Decision* (Dallas: Word Publishing, 1989).

Willard F. Harley, Jr., *His Needs, Her Needs* (Old Tappan, NJ: Fleming H. Revell Company, 1986).

Pray and ask your Father in heaven to help you be enthusiastic about being a good father.

Scripture Memory Assignment:

1 Timothy 3:8,9,12

"naked, and you clothed Me"

Matthew 25:36*a*

LESSON 4

WHAT THE OLD TESTAMENT SAYS ABOUT THE POOR AND NEEDY

Review and discuss the assignments given in lesson three.

The following Old Testament Scriptures will help you—as a deacon, wife of a deacon, or future deacon—understand God's thinking about needy people. I ask you to slowly and meditatively read the following Scriptures.

1. Every deacon must get to know Job. He is a model of godly compassion.

"Because I delivered the poor who cried for help,
And the orphan who had no helper.
The blessing of the one ready to perish came upon me,
And I made the widow's heart sing for joy.
I put on righteousness, and it clothed me;
My justice was like a robe and a turban.
I was eyes to the blind, And feet to the lame.
I was a father to the needy,
And I investigated the case which I did not know.
And I broke the jaws of the wicked,
And snatched the prey from his teeth" (Job 29:12-17).

"Have I not wept for the one whose life is hard?
Was not my soul grieved for the needy" (Job 30:25)?

"If I have kept the poor from their desire,
Or have caused the eyes of the widow to fail,
Or have eaten my morsel alone,
And the orphan has not shared it...
If I have seen anyone perish for lack of clothing,
Or that the needy had no covering,...
Let my shoulder fall from the socket,
And my arm be broken off at the elbow" (Job 31:16,17,19,22).

List the things that characterized Job's heart feelings toward the poor and needy. Next list the actions of Job's life that flowed out of these heart attitudes.

_____
_____
_____
_____
_____
_____
_____

2. Read 1 Timothy 3:13 and pages 147-150 of NTD. (a) Are the promised rewards of 1 Timothy 3:13 a proper motive for deacons to consciously seek? Why or why not? (b) Exactly who gets the rewards? (c) What precisely are the rewards? (d) How does this relate to deacons' qualifications?

_____
_____
_____
_____
_____
_____

3. An essential Old Testament passage you need to know is Deuteronomy 15:1-11, especially verses 7-11. This passage shows the heart attitudes God demands we have toward our needy brothers and sisters. The context of this chapter is the so-called Sabbath year and the cancellation of all debts [probably just for the year]: "At the end of every seven years you shall grant a remission of debts" (15:1).

If there is a poor man with you, one of your brothers, in any of your towns in your land which the Lord your God is giving you, you shall *not harden your heart, nor close your hand from your poor brother;* but you shall *freely open your hand to him, and shall generously lend him sufficient for his need* in whatever he lacks. Beware, lest there is a base thought in your heart, saying, "The seventh year, the year of remission, is near," and your eye is hostile toward your poor brother, and you give him nothing; then he may cry to the Lord against you, and it will be a sin in you. You shall generously give to him, and *your heart shall not be grieved when you give to him,* because for this thing the Lord your God will bless you in all your work and in all your undertakings (Deuteronomy 15:7-10; italics added).

What does Deuteronomy 15:7-10 have to say about the way that God expects us to give? How can we develop that kind of mentality toward giving?

_____
_____
_____
_____
_____
_____
_____
_____

4. Jeremiah (c. 646-c.586 B.C.), the tender-hearted prophet, decries the social injustice of King Jehoiakim. He also compares Jehoiakim to his godly father, King Josiah, who cared for the poor and needy. Unlike Josiah, Jehoiakim, in greed and self-interest, exploits the poor and needy to build sumptuous buildings for his own pleasure.

'Woe to him [King Jehoiakim] who builds his house without righteousness
And his upper rooms without justice,
Who uses his neighbor's services without pay
And does not give him his wages,
Who says, "I [Jehoiakim] will build myself a roomy house
With spacious upper rooms..."
Do you [Jehoiakim] become a king because you are
   competing in cedar?
Did not your father [godly King Josiah] eat and drink,
And do justice and righteousness?
Then it was well with him.

He pled the cause of the afflicted and needy;
Then it was well.
Is not that what it means to know Me?'
Declares the Lord' (Jeremiah 22:13-16; italics added).

From the above verses, what are some characteristics of godly leadership? Ponder Jeremiah 22:16. It gives us a way to measure our own relationship to God. What is it?

_____

_____

_____

_____

_____

_____

_____

5. Writing during a time of great economic prosperity but social injustice (735-710 B.C.), the prophet Micah asks: What is the heart of true religious practice? What does God demand from us?

> With what shall I come to the Lord
> And bow myself before the God on high?
> Shall I come to Him with burnt offerings,
> With yearling calves?
>
> Does the Lord take delight in thousands of rams,
> In ten thousand rivers of oil?
> Shall I present my first-born for my rebellious acts,
> The fruit of my body for the sin of my soul?
>
> He has told you, O man, what is good;
> And what does the Lord require of you,
> *But to do justice, to love kindness,*
> And to walk humbly with your God (Micah 6:6-8;
>   italics added)?

The prophet Isaiah (ministering from 740 to 680 B.C.) exposes Israel's self-righteous, religious hypocrisy. Although the people practiced outward conformity to all the external, religious rituals God had ordained, they were sinful and exceedingly selfish in their hearts and daily relationships with others. So God tells the nation the kind of religious practices He desires:

> "Why have we fasted and Thou dost not see?
> Why have we humbled ourselves and Thou dost not notice?"
>
> 'Is this not the fast which I [God] choose, To loosen the bonds of wickedness...Is it not to divide your bread with the hungry, And bring the homeless poor into the house; When you see the naked, to cover him....

And if you give yourself to the hungry, And satisfy the desire of the afflicted...Then your light will rise in darkness (Isaiah 58:3a,6a,7a,10a).

From Micah 6:6-8 and Isaiah 58:3-10 please describe what the heart of real religion is, in God's eyes. What in God's eyes is the heart of godless religion?

_____

_____

_____

_____

_____

_____

_____

6. In one of the Bible's most dramatic, piercing, and vehement chapters, Ezekiel 16, the prophet Ezekiel (c. 622-560 B.C.) compares Judah to the evil city of Sodom and states that Judah, "a bold-faced harlot," is worse than Sodom. Note the sins that God abhorred in Sodom:

'Behold, this was the guilt of your sister Sodom: she and her daughters [surrounding towns] had arrogance, abundant food, and careless ease, but *she did not help the poor and needy*. Thus they were haughty and committed abominations before Me. Therefore I removed them when I saw it' (Ezekiel 16:49,50; italics added).

List three lessons from this passage that you can apply to yourself, your church, and your nation.

_____

_____

_____

_____

_____

7. From Psalm 72:12-15, please describe what a godly leader looks like?

_____

_____

_____

Proverbs (and Psalms) has much to say about the poor and needy. Consider the following Scriptures and answer the questions.

8. Is giving to the poor saying "good-bye" to personal wealth?

- He who is gracious to a poor man lends to the Lord, and He will repay him for his good deed (Proverbs 19:17).
- He who is generous will be blessed, For he gives some of his food to the poor (Proverbs 22:9).
- How blessed is he who considers the helpless [poor] (Psalm 41:1a).

_____

_____

_____

9. What are the poor lacking?

- The poor is hated even by his neighbor. But those who love the rich are many (Proverbs 14:20).

_____

_____

10. What is the key to personal happiness?

- He who despises his neighbor [who is in need] sins, But happy is he who is gracious to the poor (Proverbs 14:21).

- He who is generous will be blessed, For he gives some of his food to the poor (Proverbs 22:9).
- How blessed is he who considers the helpless [poor] (Psalms 41:1a).

---

11. How do you honor (or reproach) God?

- He who despises his neighbor [who is in need] sins, But happy is he who is gracious to the poor (Proverbs 14:21).

---

12. How can we discover how righteous or wicked we are?

- The righteous is concerned for the rights of the poor, The wicked does not understand such concern (Proverbs 29:7).
- He who oppresses the poor reproaches his Maker, But he who is gracious to the needy honors Him (Proverbs 14:31).

---

13. How can we get ourselves into a position to be without help in a time of trouble?

- He who shuts his ear to the cry of the poor Will also cry himself and not be answered (Proverbs 21:13).

---

14. As a deacon, you will be called on to make judgments about people and their circumstances. This is a difficult job in an unjust world. When it comes to relatives and close friends, the best Christian people are guilty of bias or believing only one side of a story. From the following verses make a list of rules, promises, threats to help the deacons be able to deal with all people on the same level.

He who gives an answer before he hears, It is folly and shame to him (Proverbs 18:13).

The first to plead his case seems just, Until another comes and examines him (Proverbs 18:17).

The execution of justice is joy for the righteous (Proverbs 21:15a).

These also are sayings of the wise. To show partiality in judgment is not good (Proverbs 24:23).

You shall do no injustice in judgment; you shall not be partial to the poor nor defer to the great, but you are to judge your neighbor fairly (Leviticus 19:15).

Justice, and only justice, you shall pursue, that you may live and possess the land which the Lord your God is giving you (Deuteronomy 16:20).

And he said to the judges, "Consider what you are doing, for you do not judge for man but for the Lord who is with you when you render judgment. Now then let the fear of the Lord be upon you; be very careful what you do, for the Lord our God will have no part in unrighteousness, or partiality, or the taking of a bribe" (2 Chronicles 19:6,7).

"I was a father to the needy, And I investigated the case which I did not know" (Job 29:15).

For I, the Lord, love justice, I hate robbery in the burnt offering; And I will faithfully give them their recompense (Isaiah 61:8a).

"Our Law does not judge a man, unless it first hears from him and knows what he is doing, does it?" (John 7:51)

_____

_____

_____

_____

_____

_____

_____

_____

_____

Of the ten verses above, which two do you think you need to memorize so that you will be a better deacon? Why? (Ok, now memorize them!)

_____

_____

Personal Assignment:

A deacon must be a wise man. According to Acts 6:3, the Seven had to be full of wisdom in order to do their work effectively. I cannot think of a better way to become wise than by studying and practicing the wisdom of the Book of Proverbs. Here are some recommended books to help you in your study of Proverbs and the profound wisdom literature of the Bible.

James T. Draper, Jr., *Proverbs: Practical Directions for Living* (Wheaton: Tyndale House Publishers, 1971).

Louis Goldberg, *Savoring the Wisdom of Proverbs,* (Chicago: Moody Press, 1990).

William E. Mouser, *Getting the Most Out of Proverbs* (Grand Rapids: Zondervan Publishing House, 1991).

Derek Kidner, *The Wisdom of Proverbs, Job and Ecclesiastes* (Downers Grove: InterVarsity Press, 1985).

Charles Bridges (1794-1869), *A Modern Study in the Book of Proverbs*, revised by George F. Santa (Milford, MI: Mott Media, 1978).

Scripture Memory Assignment:

Micah 6:8

"I was thirsty, and you gave Me drink"

Matthew 25:35*b*

LESSON 5

WHAT THE NEW TESTAMENT SAYS ABOUT CARING FOR NEEDY PEOPLE, Part 1
(Read pages 25-29)

The following New Testament Scriptures will help you—as a deacon, wife of a deacon, or future deacon—understand God's thinking about needy people. I ask you to slowly and meditatively read the following Scriptures.

1. What profound truth do you learn from Matthew 25:37-40 that can revolutionize your attitude toward helping suffering, needy people?

"Lord, when did we see You hungry, and feed You, or thirsty, and give You drink? And when did we see You a stranger, and invite You in, or naked, and clothe You? And when did we see You sick, or in prison, and come to You?' And the King will answer and say to them, 'Truly I say to you, to the extent that you did it to one of these brothers of Mine, even the least of them, you did it to Me'" (Matthew 25:37-40).

2. Read the following texts carefully. As you do please make note of both the activities that they are calling for and the underlying attitudes in which these actions are to be done.

This is pure and undefiled religion in the sight of our God and Father, to visit orphans and widows in their distress, and to keep oneself unstained by the world (James 1:27).

What use is it, my brethren, if a man says he has faith, but he has no works? Can that faith save him? If a brother or sister is without clothing and in need of daily food, and one of you says to them, "Go in peace, be warmed and be filled," and yet you do not give them what is necessary for their body, what use is that? (James 2:14,15).

Now in Joppa there was a certain disciple named Tabitha (which translated in Greek is called Dorcas); this woman was abounding with deeds of kindness and charity, which she continually did (Acts 9:36).

We know love by this, that He laid down His life for us; and we ought to lay down our lives for the brethren. But whoever has the world's goods, and beholds his brother in need and closes his heart against him, how does the love of God abide in him? (1 John 3:16,17).

James and Cephas [Peter] and John, who were reputed to be pillars, gave to me [Paul] and Barnabas the right hand of fellowship, that we might go to the Gentiles, and they to the circumcised. They only asked us to remember the poor—the very thing I also was eager to do (Galatians 2:9*b*,10).

"You [elders] know that these hands ministered to my own needs and to the men who were with me. In everything I [Paul] showed you that by working hard in this manner you must help the weak and remember the words of the Lord Jesus, that He Himself said, `It is more blessed to give than to receive'" (Acts 20:35).

Now go back and in two columns make a list of what you discovered.

First and Second Thessalonians

Paul's two letters to the Thessalonians reveal some extremely important principles for deacons. You as a deacon, need to know these Scriptures, but more important, you need to know how to apply them wisely.

3. Please take a careful look at the following text. As you read it, make a list of the things that Paul is teaching the church. What is the main point he wants the church to learn? Now try to think of some ways that this point may apply to the ministry of the diaconate in the local church setting.

For you yourselves know how you ought to follow our example, because we did not act in an undisciplined manner among you, nor did we eat anyone's bread without paying for it, but with labor and hardship we kept working night and day so that we might not be a burden to any of you; not because we do not have the right to this [financial support from the church], but in order to offer ourselves as a model for you, that you might follow our example. For even when we were with you, we used to give you this order: if anyone will not work, neither let him eat (2 Thessalonians 3:7-9; also see 1 Thessalonians 2:9; Ephesians 4:28).

_____

_____

_____

_____

_____

_____

_____

_____

4. In 1 Thessalonians 4:11,12, Paul balances out loving concern for one another in the Christian community and personal responsibility to provide for one's own needs. There will always be those who will exploit Christian love. In the church at Thessalonica, for example, some were indolent, undisciplined, and irresponsible, refusing even to work (2 Thessalonians 3:6-13). They selfishly presumed on the generosity and love of their brothers and sisters. They may have become economically dependent on their Christian friends. Thus Paul makes it clear that each believer is to work and be self-sufficient:

> But we urge you, brethren, to excel still more [in love], and to make it your ambition to lead a quiet life and attend to your own business and work with your hands, just as we commanded you; so that you may behave properly toward outsiders and not be in any need (1 Thessalonians 4:10*b*-12)

Why, according to this text (and the ones in question # 3), does Paul want Christians to work to supply their own needs? (There may be more than one reason.)

_____

_____

_____

_____

_____

_____

5. When Paul lived among the new Christians at Thessalonica, he told them a number of times (as the imperfect tense of the verb "order" indicates) that those who refuse to work are not to eat at the expense of others:

> For even when we were with you, we used to give you this order [command]: if anyone will not work, neither let him eat. For we hear that some among you are leading an undisciplined life, doing no work at all, but acting like busybodies. Now such persons we command and exhort in the Lord Jesus Christ to work in quiet fashion and eat their own bread (2 Thessalonians 3:10-12).

What is Paul's advice to those who are undisciplined busybodies? Please do not simply copy Paul's words but put your answer into your own words.

_____

_____

_____

_____

_____

6. For those who persist in indolence, the Bible instructs the church to "take special note of the man and do not associate with him, so that he may be put to shame. And yet do not regard him as an enemy, but admonish him as a brother" (2 Thessalonians 3:14,15). Why do you think the Bible calls the church to treat lazy people so severely?

_____

_____

_____

_____

7. To constructively apply the biblical principle that those who refuse to work do not eat demands wisdom (something all deacons must have, Acts 6:3) and adequate facts about the person in question. This biblical principle could easily be misapplied. Innocent, needy people could be denied the material help they ought to receive. List several categories of people who do not work, but to whom the Christian community should give financial assistance.

_____

_____

_____

_____

8. Make a list of the actual ministry activity that is going on in following verses. Now make note of the heart attitudes with which this ministry was done. What were the reasons that this ministry was carried out in the way it was. Finally, try to think of some ways that this applies to the ministry of the diaconate in the local church.

And we have sent along with him the brother whose fame in the things of the gospel has spread through all the churches...he has also been appointed by the churches to travel with us in this gracious work, which is being administered by us for the glory of the Lord Himself, and to show our readiness, taking precaution that no one should discredit us in our administration of this generous gift; for we have regard for what is honorable, not only in the sight of the Lord, but also in the sight of men (2 Corinthians 8:18-21).

Assignments:

1) Mobilize people in your church who have a heart for mercy ministries. Prepare a "servant's list" of the names of people you can call on to help sick, needy, or elderly people. List people who are willing to share their homes with others, fix cars, provide transportation, visit shut-ins, make telephone calls, nurse the sick, prepare food, supervise children, read to the elderly, cut hair, clean homes, or do home repair, etc.

2) Many people are financially troubled. They need help in managing their finances. They need a plan. As deacons, you should have good books, tapes, and videos on hand to give or to recommend to people. Many people face financial difficulties because of mismanagement and undisciplined spending. Others live on small incomes, so wise financial management is essential to their survival.

Here are some books and tape series for you to investigate and have available for people to use:

Ron Blue, *The Debt Squeeze: How Your Family Can Become Financially Free* (Pamora, CA: Focus on the Family, 1989).

Larry Burkett, *Using Your Money Wisely: Biblical Principles Under Scrutiny* (Chicago: Moody Press, 1985).

Larry Burkett,*Your Finances In Changing Times,* The Christian Financial Concepts Series (Chicago:Moody Press, 1982).

Larry Burkett, *How to Manage Your Money: An In-depth Bible Study on Personal Finances* (Chicago: Moody Press, 1991).

3) In order to do some preventive medicine, see that a class on Christian financial principles is taught regularly at your church. This is a big issue for the vast majority of Christian families. Use some of the above materials for your classes.

4) For the unemployed, start a job search support group. This group can meet regularly to pray together, share information, teach job-seeking skills, and support one another during a very difficult time.

Here are some books to have on hand to give to people in this situation:

Robert N. Bolles, *What Color is Your Parachute?* (Berkeley, CA: Ten Speed Press, Box 7123, 94707). You should own several copies of this book to give to any unemployed person in your church.

Doug Sherman, *How to Keep Your Head Up When Your Job's Got You Down* (Colorado Springs: NavPress, 1989).

The Sin of Selfishness

You might as well know that the toughest foe you will face, both within the souls of others and within your own soul, is human selfishness. There are no limits to the crimes this morbid sin has committed against humanity. Selfishness is the very opposite of love. A life of selfishness is the very opposite of the life lived by Jesus Christ.

In one of the greatest books ever written on love, *Charity and Its Fruits,* Jonathan Edwards expounds on the phrase "[love] does not seek its own" (1 Corinthians 13:5*b*). To understand this verse, Edwards shows that we must go back to the Garden and the fall of the human race (Genesis 3:1-24). He gives us weighty truths to think about. Carefully read the following quotation. Edwards is often difficult to read, so in order to get the full benefit of his wisdom you might want to read the quotation twice.

The ruin that the fall brought upon the soul of man consists very much in his losing the nobler and more benevolent principles of his nature, and falling wholly under the power and government of self-love. Before, and as God created him, he was exalted, and noble, and generous; but now he is debased, and ignoble, and selfish. Immediately upon the fall, the mind of man shrank from its primitive greatness and expandedness, to an exceeding smallness and contractedness;...Before, his soul was under the government of that noble principle of divine love, whereby it was enlarged to the comprehension of all his fellow-creatures and their welfare...But so soon as he had transgressed against God, these noble principles were immediately lost, and all this excellent enlargedness of man's soul was gone; and thenceforward he himself shrank, as it were, into a little space circumscribed and closely shut up within itself, to the exclusion of all things else. Sin, like some powerful astringent, contracted his soul to the very small dimensions of selfishness; and God was forsaken, and fellow-creatures forsaken, and man retired within himself, and became totally governed by narrow and selfish principles and feelings. Self-love became absolute master of his soul, and the more noble and spiritual principles of his being took wings and flew

73

away (*Charity and its Fruits*, [1852; repr. Edinburgh: The Banner of Truth Trust, 1978], pp. 157,158).

9. Using Edwards' vivid and powerful descriptions of fallen human nature from the above quotation, list at least three descriptions that best describe the human qualities that exist in fallen, sinful people.

a. _____

b. _____

c. _____

10. Underline what you think is the most vivid phrase from Edwards' quotation that summarizes the self-centered nature of the human heart.

_____

_____

_____

_____

_____

_____

11. Based on Edwards' quotation, what should be the predominant characteristics of a born-again child of God.

_____

_____

_____

_____

_____

_____

Practical Suggestions to Discuss:

1) Every church should have a food pantry. This is a very simple, practical way of helping people in financial need. It is also an excellent way of involving and teaching adults and children about caring for needy people. Families should be encouraged to regularly share their food or finances with the food pantry (Acts 4:34,35). In order to run an effective food pantry contact organizations or churches that have a successful program.

2) Consider starting a clothing closet.

3) You may know of Christians in prison. They need to be remembered and helped (Hebrews 13:3). You can do many practical things to encourage them.

4) Many elderly people need help in understanding tax questions, insurance policies, medical papers, government agencies, and wills. You can organize a free counseling service for the elderly utilizing Christian businessmen, tax consultants, insurance men, and nurses.

Scripture Memory Assignment:

2 Corinthians 8:3-5

"I was in prison, and you came to Me"

Matthew 25:36*c*

LESSON 6

WHAT THE NEW TESTAMENT SAYS ABOUT CARING FOR NEEDY PEOPLE, Part 2

Review and discuss the assignments given in lesson five.

1. There is an old saying, "Man before business, 'cause man is your business." How does this saying apply to deacons?

_____

_____

_____

_____

2. As you read through the following verses make note of the actions that some believers engaged in on behalf of others. What heart attitudes gave rise to such activities?

> For there was not a needy person among them, for all who were owners of land or houses would sell them and bring the proceeds of the sales, and lay them at the apostles' feet; and they would be distributed to each, as any had need (Acts 4:34,35).

And one of them named Agabus stood up [in the church in Antioch] and began to indicate by the Spirit that there would certainly be a great famine all over the world.... And in the proportion that any of the disciples had means, each of them determined to send a contribution for the relief of the brethren living in Judea. And this they did, sending it in charge of Barnabas and Saul to the elders (Acts 11:28a; 29,30).

Now, brethren, we wish to make known to you the grace of God which has been given in the churches of Macedonia, that in a great ordeal of affliction their abundance of joy and their deep poverty overflowed in the wealth of their liberality. For I testify that according to their ability, and beyond their ability they gave of their own accord, begging us with much entreaty for the favor of participation in the support of the saints [the poor saints in Jerusalem] (2 Corinthians 8:1-4).

For Macedonia and Achaia have been pleased to make a contribution for the poor among the saints in Jerusalem (Romans 15:26).

_____
_____
_____
_____
_____

3. What is the goal of Paul's advice in the following passage of Scripture?

For this [the offering for the poor in Jerusalem] is not for the ease of others and for your affliction, but by way of equality—at this present time your [the Christians in Corinth] abundance being a supply for their [the church in Jerusalem] want, that their abundance also may become a supply for your want, that there may be equality (2 Corinthians 8:13,14).

_____

_____

_____

_____

_____

4. As the ministers of mercy, the deacons are to be living models of Christian mercy and financial responsibility. From the following verses, make a list of the attitudes and mindset as well as the lifestyle and actions that should characterize deacons as living models of Christian behavior as it relates to money and material possessions.

Let him who steals steal no longer; but rather let him labor, performing with his own hands what is good, in order that he may have something to share with him who has need (Ephesians 4:28).

Instruct those who are rich in this present world...to do good, to be rich in good works, to be generous and ready to share, storing up for themselves the treasure of a good foundation for the future (1 Timothy 6:17a,18,19a).

Contributing to the needs of the saints (Romans 12:13a).

For we have brought nothing into the world, so we cannot take anything out of it either. And if we have food and covering, with these we shall be content (1 Timothy 6:7,8).

Let your character be free from the love of money, being content with what you have (Hebrews 13:5a).

And do not neglect doing good and sharing; for with such sacrifices God is pleased (Hebrews 13:16).

Do not lay up for yourselves treasures upon earth, where moth and rust destroy, and where thieves break in and steal. But lay up for yourselves treasures in heaven, where neither moth nor rust destroys, and where thieves do not break in or steal; for where your treasure is, there will your heart be also (Matthew 6:19-21).

_____

_____

_____

_____

_____

_____

_____

First Timothy 5:3-16

For deacons, 1 Timothy 5:3-16 is a critically important passage. It contains invaluable, guiding principles for the local church, individuals, families, or widows. Please read this passage carefully and become very familiar with it:

Honor widows who are widows indeed (verse 3);

but if any widow has children or grandchildren, let them first learn to practice piety in regard to their own family, and to make some return to their parents; for this is acceptable in the sight of God (verse 4).

Now she who is a widow indeed, and who has been left alone has fixed her hope on God, and continues in entreaties and prayers night and day (verse 5).

Now she who gives herself to wanton pleasure is dead even while she lives (verse 6).

Prescribe these things as well, so that they may be above reproach (verse 7).

But if anyone does not provide for his own, and especially for those of his household, he has denied the faith, and is worse than an unbeliever (verse 8).

Let a widow be put on the list only if she is not less than sixty years old, having been the wife of one man, having a reputation for good works; and if she has brought up children, if she has shown hospitality to strangers, if she has washed the saints' feet, if she has assisted those in distress, and if she has devoted herself to every good work (verses 9,10).

But refuse to put younger widows on the list, for when they feel sensual desires in disregard of Christ, they want to get married, thus incurring condemnation, because they have set aside their previous pledge. And at the same time they also learn to be idle, as they go around from house to house; and not merely idle, but also gossips and busybodies, talking about things not proper to mention. Therefore, I want younger widows to get married, bear children, keep house, and give the enemy no occasion for reproach; for some have already turned aside to follow Satan (verses 11-15).

If any woman who is a believer has dependent widows, let her assist them, and let not the church be burdened, so that it may assist those who are widows indeed (verse 16).

Special Note:

The church in Ephesus had a special widows' roll (a list or register of widows' names). The roll consisted of widows whom the church was responsible to protect and financially support. The problem was, too many unqualified widows were placed on the church's roll. This unduly burdened the church financially (verse 16b) and actually harmed some of the widows (verses 11- 15). Paul seeks to correct this abuse.

The main point of Paul's instruction is clear: not every widow qualifies to be on the church's widows' roll. The church is responsible primarily for truly destitute, godly, elderly widows (verses 5,9,10).

Paul emphatically makes the point that individual Christian families—not the local church—should be responsible to care for their family members who are widows (verses 4 and 8). Of 1 Timothy 5:3-16, Oxford scholar, J. N. D. Kelly writes, 'But the repetition, and the Apostle's sharper tone, may underline his exasperation at the selfishness of some families in the Ephesian church' (*The Pastoral Epistles,* [London: Adam and Charles Black, 1972] p.115).

Furthermore, younger widows (verses 11-15) should not be placed on the widows' roll because their status as enrolled widows may expose them to difficult temptations. Their placement on the widows' roll could result in terrible harm to their spiritual commitment to Christ, a tragedy that had already happened to some of the younger widows (verse 15).

We should not, however, falsely conclude that because a widow, young or old, does not meet all the qualifications of verses 9 and 10 that the local church can forego helping such a person. The point of verses 9 and 10 is that only certain widows should be placed on the widows' roll, a status that guarantees the church's full guardianship and financial aid.

Finally, some commentators believe that this passage speaks of a distinct order of widows who vow to serve the church and remain widows throughout life, for which they receive material aid and official status. I find this interpretation highly unlikely.

5. What does Paul mean by the designation "widows indeed"?

_____

_____

_____

6. Why does the Lord have a special regard for widows?

_____

_____

_____

7. There is a family financial responsibility discussed in verse 4. Please describe it in detail?

_____

_____

_____

8. In light of all the problems in the church in Ephesus (pages 84,85 in the NTD), what does Paul mean in verse 4 by the statement, "Let them first learn to practice piety in regard to their own family"?

_____

_____

_____

_____

_____

9. As a deacon, you must understand and master the biblical principles taught in verses 4 and 5. Can you explain how these verses should guide deacons in situations in which people ask for money or food? Can you think of any examples?

_____
_____
_____
_____
_____
_____
_____

10. What criteria does Scripture give to guide the local church knowing which widows it is *not obligated* to support fully? See 1 Timothy 5:4,6,8,11-12,16.

_____
_____
_____
_____
_____

11. What level of financial support does 1 Timothy 5:16*b* envision the local church providing for "widows indeed"?

_____
_____
_____
_____

12. After reading *The New Testament Deacon* how have your ideas about deacons changed? Explain your answer!

_____
_____
_____
_____

Scripture Memory Assignment:

1 Timothy 5:8.

FUTURE DISCUSSION PLANNING SHEET

FUTURE DISCUSSION PLANNING SHEET

FUTURE DISCUSSION PLANNING SHEET

_____

_____

_____

_____

_____

_____

_____

_____

_____

_____

_____

_____

_____

_____

_____

_____

_____

_____

_____

_____

_____

_____

_____

_____

_____

FUTURE DISCUSSION PLANNING SHEET

_____

_____

_____

_____

_____

_____

_____

_____

_____

_____

_____

_____

_____

_____

_____

_____

_____

_____

_____

_____

_____

_____

_____

_____

FUTURE DISCUSSION PLANNING SHEET

FUTURE DISCUSSION PLANNING SHEET

FUTURE DISCUSSION PLANNING SHEET

Leading with Love
by Alexander Strauch

If you lead or teach people--whether as a Sunday School teacher, youth worker, women's or men's ministry leader, Bible study leader, administrator, music director, elder, deacon, pastor, missionary or evangelist--this book will help you become a more loving leader or teacher. A study guide is also available. Go to www.lewisandroth.org to view sample chapters.

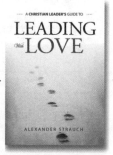

--- A CHRISTIAN LEADER'S GUIDE TO ---
LEADING with LOVE

ALEXANDER STRAUCH

"This message is urgently needed by all of us. You may have many talents and spiritual gifts, but without the love that this book speaks about, you don't really have much at all."

-- *George Verwer, Founder, Operation Mobilization*

"*Leading with Love* demonstrates that love is indispensable for effective spiritual leadership. I hope this insightful study will receive the enthusiatic response it deserves and that it will be widely read."

-- *Dr. Vernon Grounds, Chancellor, Denver Seminary*

Oops! I Forgot My Wife
by Doyle Roth

If you're looking for a different kind of marriage book, this is it! Using humor, a true-to-life case study and solid Biblical instruction, *Oops! I Forgot My Wife* weaves together a fun and easy-to-read story that helps couples see themselves and their marriages from a fresh perspective.

Written as an exchange of emails between a church elder and a young man whose marriage is crash landing, *Oops!* features short chapters and a straight-talk style that hits the issues head on. In addition, it:

- Equips men for spiritual leadership in the home
- Challenges marriages to face their #1 enemy: self-centeredness
- Encourages friends and mentors to intentionally "bear one another's burdens"
- Provides a helpful resource for counseling, discipleship and group study with a quick, no-homework discussion guide
- Creates a "user-friendly" approach for evangelism

Study Guide and Audio Book also available.

View sample chapters online at www.lewisandroth.org.

Agape Leadership
by Alexander Strauch

This small (76 pages) but powerful book features twelve leadership lessons drawn from the life of Robert Chapman. Chapman, described by C. H. Spurgeon as "the saintliest man I ever knew," determined early in his life not only to preach Christ, but to live Christ. In the years that followed, Chapman's reputation grew to legendary proportions on account of his kindness, balanced judgment, ability to reconcile conflict, and loving pastoral care.

"It will challenge you to be a better leader, a more committed believer, and a brighter light to the world."
-- *Greg Stephenson, Grace Community Church, Grace Ministries International*

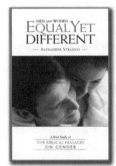

Men and Women: Equal Yet Different
by Alexander Strauch

Written for those who want to know more about the biblical teachings on gender but don't have time to read lengthy tomes on the subject, this small book is also perfect for high school and college students. It addresses one of the most significant changes that has occurred in human history: the gender revolution. Like the rest of society, Christianity has been permanently affected by this change. *Men and Women: Equal Yet Different* presents the complementarian perspective that men and women are equal yet different, and introduces the key terms, arguments, Scripture passages, and research related to this position. Each chapter includes questions for group study.

"...[Strauch] stands squarely on the side of historical Christianity with his basic presentation of male-female issues..."
-- *John MacArthur, Jr., Pastor, Grace Community Church*

"...[this] volume...is strategically important. [It] gives an introduction to the subject that offers clear and easily understood information for the lay person as well as challenging considerations for the scholar."
-- *Dorothy Patterson, Professor of Theology in Women's Studies, Southwestern Baptist Theological Seminary*

"...*Men and Women: Equal Yet Different* lets the Bible speak for itself in the clearest of terms."
-- *R. Kent Hughes, Pastor, College Church*

Biblical Eldership
by Alexander Strauch

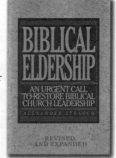

With over 150,000 copies sold, this comprehensive look at the role and function of elders brings all the advantages of shared leadership into focus. Written for those seeking a clear understanding of the mandate for biblical eldership, this book defines it accurately, practically and according to Scripture.

"Mr. Strauch has made a fine contribution to the subject of eldership. I am confident that it will be helpful to many.

-- John MacArthur, Pastor, Grace Community Church

"A very useful resource for teaching the New Testament truth regarding elders in the local church. Sound, clear, and extremely important. Recommended."

-- Reformation & Revival Journal

"Our eldership has gone through *Biblical Eldership* and the guide book twice. It has been the finest investment of our time in the twelve years that I've been at the church. *Biblical Eldership* is a fine work and a thorough Biblical exposition on eldership."

-- Bryce Jessup, President, William Jessup University

"At last, a thorough biblical study on the basis of church government and especially the function and ministry of elders! New churches will find it a valuable guideline to effective functioning and older churches will find it a trustworthy corrective."

Ray Stedman, former Pastor, Peninsula Bible Church

ALSO AVAILABLE:
Biblical Eldership Study Guide
Biblical Eldership Mentor's Guide
Biblical Eldership Booklet (abridged)
Biblical Eldership Discussion Guide

Lewis & Roth Publishers
800.477.3239
www.lewisandroth.org